BRITAIN
YESTERDAY & TODAY

THIS IS A CARLTON BOOK

Design copyright © 2003, 2005, 2012 Carlton Publishing Group
Text copyright © 2003, 2005, 2012 Janice Anderson
& Edmund Swinglehurst

This edition published in 2012 by Carlton Books Ltd
A Division of the Carlton Publishing Group
20 Mortimer Street
London
W1T 3JW

First published in 2003

A CIP catalogue for this book is available from the British Library.

ISBN 978 1 78097 088 2

BRITAIN
YESTERDAY & TODAY

Janice Anderson & Edmund Swinglehurst

CARLTON
BOOKS

CONTENTS

FOREWORD BY PETER SISSONS

What is it about Britain that makes the images in this book so evocative, and so important historically?

'Typical British' is one of the most over-used phrases, and not just in the English language. For me, what lies at the heart of this phrase is our greatest national treasure: freedom of expression. In Britain this freedom is the mother of every other national characteristic — especially inventiveness, ingenuity and tolerance.

The British are adaptable and adventurous. They are excited by things that are new, but they don't trust them until they are tried and tested. The story of Britain is the story of steady change.

For well over a hundred years now, since reliable photography became commonplace, we've been able to record that change — and the pictures are fascinating across the whole of British life.

The British are a sporting nation, and the great fixtures of the sporting year — Wimbledon, Cup Final, Lords, Twickenham and Boat Race — are national institutions; but they've changed. The British enjoy their leisure, and have always believed they're entitled to it, whatever hand life has dealt them, but they'll change their habits, if it's change for the better.

They enjoy their entertainment too. In the late fifties, a new generation — not yet slaves to TV and the Internet — made their own entertainment, and British popular music caught the imagination of young and old across the world.

The British still value the concept of fair play. Their political parties vie with each other in promising social improvement and the alleviation of hardship. It's a national pastime to complain about how slowly social conditions change, but change they do. The centres of most of our great cities bear eloquent witness.

A Briton's home is his castle, and improvements to both home and garden — if you believe the TV schedulers — border on a national obsession.

The British are also a fighting nation. Two world wars, and many lesser conflicts, have left their scars and their badges of pride.

The Britain of yesterday was different, but it made Britain what it is today. Inside these pages you'll see what I mean....

Peter

INTRODUCTION

The United Kingdom of Great Britain and Northern Ireland has much to be proud of and much to celebrate. We pack into a comparatively small space some of the world's most beautiful countryside, where rolling green and gold farmland and 'blue remembered hills' are studded with lakes, lochs and tarns and watered by great rivers and sparkling streams. Our towns and cities include some that are among the most architecturally handsome and innovative in the world. Our society is essentially peaceful and well ordered, set on a firmly democratic base in which we all have a say, through the ballot box, in what goes on nationally and at a local level.

Things are not like this for many other countries in the world, and they were not always like this for us. Britain yesterday – in the nineteenth and early twentieth centuries – was an imperial

power and a nation that relied on its industries, most of them in the Midlands and the north of England, for most of its great wealth and for the income of the bulk of its people. Today, sociologists and historians tell us, we are a post-industrial society, whose once-mighty industrial base has dwindled to a shadow of its former might and in which an entirely different kind of economy, based on 'invisible earnings' and service industries, directs the way in which we live our lives and choose the ways by which we earn our living.

During the move from an industrial world to a post-industrial one, our standards of living improved dramatically, though not without many difficulties. Today, the welfare of the individual is an essential concern, education is a universal right, adult men and women all have the vote, and many kinds of leisure can be enjoyed by everyone in the free time that shorter working hours and longer paid holidays have given us.

All this has happened during a time when science and technology have progressed at breathtaking speed. On the way, they have given us steam propulsion of many kinds – including railways and ships – the telegraph, electric light, sewage systems, paved roads, the internal combustion engine, powered flight, radio communications and many, many more benefits, most of which were little more than a gleam in scientists' eyes when Prince Albert opened the Great Exhibition in London's Hyde Park in 1851.

Today, Britain is again one of the world's most prosperous nations. It is a country where the bulk of the population, who once rarely saw foreign faces, now lives in a multi-ethnic society where many races and religions live together in remarkable peace and harmony. It is a country whose people, who once ate mostly roast beef or boiled mutton, are now connoisseurs of pasta, pizza, Peking duck, vindaloo curry, sushi and chilli con carne. And it is a country where people still happily celebrate centuries-old traditions and customs in the midst of twenty-first-century technology and wizardry.

This book is a celebration of all these aspects of life in Britain today, and of the adaptability, ingenuity and tolerance of the British people.

FREE TIME 1

GREAT DAYS OUT

Before the railway age, days off were spent
locally for most Britons, if they took them at
all. The train enabled people to get away
quickly to the countryside and the seaside. The
1871 Bank Holidays Act, which established the
Easter, Whitsun, August and Christmas bank
holidays, gave another fillip to the idea of
taking a short break from home and work.

The seaside was the most popular
destination for days out in Britain and all the
big resorts catered as much for the day visitor
as for the longer-term holidaymaker. Margate
and Southend, downriver from London,
Brighton on the south coast and Blackpool in
the north were among the most popular
resort towns.

While a trip to the seaside is still a great day
out, more sophisticated day trippers have their
search for excitement met by all the fun of the
theme park. The great theme parks, such as
Alton Towers in Staffordshire and Thorpe Park
in Surrey, offer a dazzling array of rides,
entertainment and other attractions that
quieter suppliers of great days out, such as the
National Trust, cannot match.

1939
Holidaymakers on two-seater bicycles
carry out a friendly invasion of
Clacton-on-Sea's Marine Parade from
Butlins Holiday Camp in the town.

HOLIDAY CAMPS

Billy Butlin launched the first of his many
holiday camps at Skegness in 1936 and one at
Clacton-on-Sea two years later. His camps and
those people who followed him, such as the
holiday giant Thomas Cook, provided clean,
simple holiday accommodation in wood cabins
at a time when life was hard for many.

After the war was over in 1945, holiday
camps were hugely popular, offering all kinds of
entertainments and fun for all ages, from
knobbly-knees competitions and bathing-
beauty pageants to ballroom dancing and light
entertainment, day and night.

The advent of the cheap package holiday
abroad in the 1960s meant the end of the old-
style Butlins camp. People wanted freedom, not
the constant attention of regiments of
blazered hosts making everyone 'join in'.

Today's holiday camp is a very different
being. It is called a 'holiday leisure resort' and
it is built with the British weather in mind. At
Center Parcs, for instance, visitors can indulge
in water sports and games in a sub-tropical
climate, oblivious of any snow or rain outside.

TODAY
The swimming pool, complete with
tropical palms and a poolside coffee
bar, at the Center Parcs holiday
resort in Longleat in Wiltshire.

TATE MODERN

The transformation of Bankside Power Station on the south bank of the Thames into Tate Modern began in 1995. The art gallery was opened in the millennium year, 2000, but the footbridge that was meant to link it to the north bank near St Paul's Cathedral had to be closed because it swung too much. It opened to the public in 2002, since when it has been a hugely popular way of reaching the gallery.

The Bankside Power Station, designed by architect Sir Giles Gilbert Scott, was built in two phases between 1947 and 1963. It is a brick-clad steel structure, with some 4.2 million bricks used in its construction. The main chimney was kept down to a height of 99 metres (325 feet) so that it would be lower that Christopher Wren's dome on St Paul's.

The building was transformed into a truly exciting gallery of modern art by world-famous Swiss architects Herzog & de Meuron. Their greatest change was to add a two-storey glass structure spanning the length of the roof, which lets natural light into the galleries and houses a café offering spectacular panoramic views across London.

1877
The elegant party picnicking at
Stonehenge includes Queen Victoria's
son, Prince Leopold, Duke of Albany
(reclining on his elbow, cigar in hand).

MYSTERIOUS STONEHENGE

The great circle of stones called Stonehenge
that stands in a field on the Salisbury Plain in
Wiltshire is one of the most important
survivals from pre-historic times in Britain. It
has long attracted thousands of visitors every
year, not least those seeking some remnant of
the sun-worshipping Druids.

Druids held sun-worshipping ceremonies at
Stonehenge nearly four thousand years ago.
Today, Companions of the Most Ancient Order
of Druids keep vigil at Stonehenge every
21 June, the day of the summer solstice.

Wear and tear caused by the huge numbers
of visitors to the site led English Heritage to
come up with a major redevelopment plan in
2010. Their plan to create a new visitor centre,
incorporating a high-quality exhibition and
education centre set well away from
Stonehenge itself and linked to it by a visitor
transit system, was approved by Wiltshire
Council but was still encountering opposition
several years on.

TODAY
Police were present in strength in
2001 at a revival of the ancient
Druids' way of celebrating the
summer solstice at Stonehenge.

1929

Fans queue round the block at the Astoria in Brixton, south London, to see variety entertainer Al Jolson's second 'talkie', *The Singing Fool*.

THE CINEMA

Moving pictures were first shown in Britain in darkened halls, variety theatres, fairgrounds and 'penny gaffs'. The first cinemas – with padded seats, fluted columns and potted ferns, and a pianist or even a musical trio in attendance – gave way in the twenties to a wonderful riot of styles, from Spanish and Mexican to Art Deco and 'Odeon' modernist.

Cinema-going in Britain today, with ticket sales soaring, is very different. The cinema is more likely to be a vast, multi-screen complex on the edge of town than a theatre-like building on the high street. Movie-goers, with tickets bought via phone or the Internet, park within yards of the entrance, arm themselves with buckets of popcorn and other delights, and settle in seats like armchairs to have their senses assaulted by the effects of the latest computer-generated film technology.

Cinemas now also show live performances by satellite from such major arts venues as Britain's National Theatre and the New York Metropolitan Opera. These have proved immensely popular. Cinema-going is once again as exciting, and even as glamorous, as it was in the thirties, when it first became a major part of the national culture.

TODAY

One of the multi-screen cinemas which helps to meet modern cinema demands. This one, which is in Maidenhead in Berkshire, is part of the Odeon chain.

PLAYING IN THE PARK

Providing fresh air and fun for children became
an objective of early Victorian town planners,
horrified by the appalling conditions in which
so many people in Britain's towns lived.

Increasing numbers of parks and gardens,
hitherto usually privately owned, were opened
for everyone to enjoy. Manchester, for instance,
opened three public parks in 1846, all paid for
by public subscription. One of them, Peel Park,
included among the trees and flowerbeds
swings and see-saws for children and areas set
aside for ninepins, bowls and gymnastics.

Play areas in parks still have a big part to
play in children's well-being. The fight today is
against the results of affluence. Too much fast
food, too much sitting in front of TV and
computer screens and too little exercise is
making children fat. The brightly painted,
cleverly designed play areas are there to
attract children away from their television and
computer screens and out into the park.

TODAY
Children have fun in a colourful,
well-designed play area in Moors
Valley Country Park, near Ringwood
in Hampshire.

LOWRY'S WORLD

Although a city in its own right, with a charter granted in 1230 and an important part played in the creation of Britain's industrial wealth, Salford has become almost submerged in the urban sprawl of Greater Manchester.

This once-grimy centre of industry became a big star in the arts firmament when the Lowry arts complex was opened at Salford Quays. L S Lowry, who was born in Salford in 1887, began his working life as a clerk but soon turned to art, training in Manchester. In hundreds of drawings and paintings he recorded the life of the Lancashire industrial scene. Many of his paintings are peopled with ant-like crowds of stick figures scurrying among factories and grimy buildings. He was made a Royal Academician in 1962 in recognition of his unique contribution to art.

The Lowry was built in 1999 with the help of a £64 million grant from National Lottery funding. Set in the heart of the re-developed Salford Quays, the Lowry is a centre for performing and visual arts and the place to go to see some of L S Lowry's finest work in the world that inspired it.

IN THE GARDEN

'Our England is a garden ... full of borders, beds and shrubberies,' wrote Rudyard Kipling. His countrymen tried to emulate nature rather than formalize it, in the Continental style, in their home gardens. Herbaceous borders were planted with tall hollyhocks, lupins and delphiniums, while petunias, carnations and pansies spilled over onto paths. Pergolas draped with honeysuckle, rambler roses and clematis provided gardens with private areas where ladies, wearing bonnets to protect their faces from the sun, could enjoy moments of quiet.

Until the mid-twentieth century, gardeners were widely employed, but rising wages and alternative job opportunities caused their disappearance. Today, everyone is their own gardener. Inspired by TV gardeners, at weekends they head for garden centres, which have blossomed under the influence of television, radio and newspaper gardening experts.

The Chelsea Flower Show has been a top gardening (and social) event since its inception in 1913. Today's show runs for five days, and on the last day everything is sold off to the garden-loving public.

TODAY
Traditional English garden design often gives way to a futuristic world view at the Chelsea Flower Show, as in this garden from a recent show.

1937
Escaping an August heatwave, this angler, still in his working suit, lets one of his three rods look after itself while he dozes among the bulrushes.

ANGLING

The soothing experience of a day's fishing has been enjoyed by country folk and townspeople alike for centuries. Enthusiasm for the pastime grew in the nineteenth century and steps toward its regulation began. For the better-off, land-owning classes, fishing meant fishing for salmon and trout on private stretches of rivers. The ordinary fish of rivers and streams, such as perch, carp and pike, provided coarse fishing for everyone else.

Village shops near rivers began to carry stocks of rods, reels, lines and floats. Specialist shops were opened and the first angling magazines were published, giving advice on how and where to fish.

Today, a licence is always needed for anyone fishing for salmon and trout. Coarse fishing on streams and rivers usually requires a water-authority licence, too, but the fee is modest and easily obtained. Many anglers opt for fishing specially stocked, privately run lakes and reservoirs. Wherever the setting, outwitting the wily denizens of inland waters is always a challenge for the fisherman's patience.

TODAY
The green umbrellas sheltering these Thames anglers are a familiar sight along riverbanks and around lakes and reservoirs in Britain.

1935
A low-flying Hawker Hart biplane gives the crowd a hair-parting thrill at an airshow at the Hendon airfield in north London.

FUN IN THE AIR

Taking to the air in a flying machine caught the public imagination in the 1920s. Pilots from the Royal Flying Corps (re-named the Royal Air Force in 1918) found new work at airshows, demonstrating the capabilities of the biplanes that had taken part in the First World War and even offering aerial flips for a few shillings.

Much of this kind of flying was done from farm fields, or from the long, flat beaches of resorts such as Tenby in Wales. Flying displays were regular events at two former military airfields in London, Hendon and Northolt.

As flying became more commonplace, simply going up into the air for a few minutes lost its attraction. From 1948, the public's greater expectations were met for 50 years by the annual Farnborough Air Show, with its flying displays at the frontiers of technology. At the same time, fine air museums such as the Royal Air Force Museum at Hendon and the Imperial War Museum's air museum at Duxford in Cambridgeshire were taking shape. Today, their displays, in the air and on the ground, recreate the thrill of flying for everyone.

TODAY
After the marriage in April 2011 of Prince William and Kate Middleton, the RAF staged a flypast over Buckingham Palace, led by a Spitfire, a Lancaster bomber and a Hurricane.

1892
The Temperate House at Kew Gardens was opened in 1860. By 1892, the house's central walk was dwarfed by its plants.

GREAT BOTANIC GARDENS

The world's first horticultural garden began as a private botanic garden laid out along the Thames in the grounds of Kew Palace by Augusta, Princess of Wales in the 1750s.

Today, the Royal Botanic Gardens at Kew is a major horticultural and botanic institution and a fine public garden. Among Kew's many attractions are several glasshouses, ranging from Decimus Burton's great Palm House of 1848 to the Princess of Wales Conservatory, named after Princess Augusta and opened by Diana, Princess of Wales in 1987.

Since 2000, Kew's glasshouses have been rivalled for garden lovers' attention by the giant domes, called biomes, of the Eden Project in Cornwall. Essentially a conservatory of the world's ecological systems, the Eden Project attracts some two million visitors a year to its two biomes, devoted to the humid tropics and the warm temperate zone. In 2006 the Queen opened a third biome, The Core, an educational centre providing the visitor with a deeper understanding into 'learning to live with the grain of nature'.

TODAY
Dawn breaks above the humid tropics biome at the Eden Project, built in a disused china-clay pit near St Austell in Cornwall.

CYCLING

The invention of the safety bicycle with a
protected chain guard in the 1870s brought
the age of universal cycling into being. Even
Prime Minister Gladstone approved, saying that
cycling offered almost unbounded benefits,
physically, morally and socially.

Mr Gladstone had only men in mind, but
soon women were as enthusiastic cyclists as
men, the 'new women' among them going as
far as adopting the American Mrs Amelia
Bloomer's splendid trousers for cycling wear.
For the Victorian man, the cycling club became
a major attraction of the weekends. Men liked
the competitive aspect of the cycling club,
which included cycling round specially built
oval circuits and taking part in long-distance
cross-country rallies.

The present-day popularity of leisure-time
cycling, spurred on by the invention of the
mountain bike, has led to the building of a
National Cycle Network, which will eventually
cover the country. By 2010, the network's
fifteenth anniversary, it had grown to 21,000
kilometres (13,000 miles) over a mixture of
traffic-free routes, quiet lanes and traffic-
calmed city streets.

TODAY
Two helmeted cyclists on mountain
bikes splash through a ford on a
forest track near Ballachulish in the
Scottish Highlands.

ESSENTIALLY BRITISH 2

1880

Unused bathing machines and well-clad people suggest there's a cool breeze blowing on the beach at Pensarn in Colwyn Bay, Wales.

AT THE SEASIDE

By the end of the Edwardian age, mixed bathing had become acceptable at Britain's seaside resorts. Only the most modest woman felt the need to step into the sea from the steps of a bathing machine that had been dragged into the briny by a horse.

The bathing machines, which had been a feature of every English seaside resort since the mid-eighteenth century, were damp, dark and smelly and were not much missed. Many of them had their huge wheels removed and were converted into huts – the provision of shelter being particularly welcome given the unpredictable English summer weather.

Modern beach huts are a much-loved amenity and many of them, being privately owned, fetch large sums when sold. More than just somewhere to change out of wet bathing costumes and store the beach equipment, the modern beach hut may have all the amenities of a summer house, often well furnished and with electricity for lighting and making a cup of tea. The British seaside resorts may have stiff competition from Continental beaches, but they remain very popular.

TODAY

Brightly painted beach huts, some of which may be old bathing machines, are among the amenities of Southwold beach, Suffolk.

It is 21 June, and the parish of St Botolph in Bishopsgate, London, celebrates the summer solstice by dancing round a maypole.

DANCING ROUND THE MAYPOLE

Pagans danced round trees as part of a tree-worshipping ritual. In Christian times, the worship of nature turned into a celebration of its life-giving force on May Day and at the summer solstice in June. The tree was replaced by a be-ribboned pole for young people to dance round.

Dancing round maypoles – like that other medieval custom, morris dancing – is still very popular in smaller towns and villages. It is a regular feature of primary-school fetes, the children putting many hours of practice into getting their dancing right, so that their ribbons wrap themselves in a colourful pattern round the pole.

Since it became an official UK bank holiday, May Day itself is often celebrated in a style more akin to medieval revelry than decorous primary-school dancing. May Day again sees young people letting their hair down and dancing in the streets.

TODAY

May Day 2002. These anti-capitalist demonstrators have opted to use the bank holiday to march – and dance – in protest through London.

1935
Shoppers and workers queue at a
van at London's Caledonian Market
for a portion of fish and chips,
wrapped in newspaper.

FISH AND CHIPS

The railway relieved Britain's long-standing
problem of how to supply cheap food to urban
workers by quickly moving plentiful supplies of
fish from fishing harbours to the towns. Fish
and chips, bought for a few pence, sprinkled
with vinegar and wrapped in cornets made
from the daily newspaper, became the favourite
meal of the urban working classes.

The supremacy of the fish supper was not
challenged until quite late in the twentieth
century. Cheap package holidays introduced
millions of Britons to different kinds of food at
a time when Indian and Chinese food, the
hamburger and the hot dog were all beginning
to cast their spells over British high streets.

Then the cod, haddock, whiting and plaice
that were the essentials of the fish and chip
business became scarce and expensive. Fish
and chips lost its place as Britain's top dish. It
is still a very popular meal, however, as fish and
chip impresario Harry Ramsden has
successfully demonstrated. His restaurants do
great business from Blackpool to Brighton,
from Heathrow to Hong Kong.

TODAY
Fish and chips are as popular as ice
cream at this stall on one of the
three piers at Blackpool, the north
of England's favourite resort.

1926
A left-hander, the Duke of York – later George VI – took part in the doubles in the 1926 Championships, partnered by Commander Greig.

WIMBLEDON

The first Wimbledon tennis championships, all-Englishmen affairs, were held in 1877, on the grounds of the All-England Croquet Club. Players from overseas, first from the United States then from Australia and New Zealand, began taking part from the late 1880s.

Although tennis players began changing from amateurs to professionals in the 1920s in America, it was not until 1968 that Wimbledon, one of the world's four 'grand slam' tournaments, was opened to amateur and professional players alike. This move, helped by the arrival of colour television bounced off satellites to every country in the world, turned tennis into today's multimillion-dollar business in which the stars of the game can quickly become wealthy celebrities.

Wimbledon is the only grand slam tennis tournament played on grass. So crowded is the sport's calendar today that in 2003 Wimbledon was moved back a week to allow more time for players to adjust from playing on the French championship's clay to tackling the former Victorian croquet club's lawn.

TODAY
Petra Kvitova of the Czech Republic on her way to winning the Ladies' final against Russian Maria Sharapova at Wimbledon in 2011.

1905
Beatrix Potter at the door of Hill Top, her Lake District home and the setting for many of her delightful children's stories.

NATIONAL TRUST

Among the many organizations in the UK concerned with protecting the environment, the National Trust and the National Trust for Scotland stand out as charities that protect and conserve both buildings of historic interest and areas of natural beauty.

Founded in 1895, the NT acquired its first property, Alfriston Clergy House in Sussex, in 1896. Today, it looks after 255,000 hectares (30,000 acres) of land in England, Wales and Northern Ireland, on which stand 200 historic houses, 160 gardens, 40,000 ancient monuments and archaeological remains and 46 villages. Over the border, the National Trust for Scotland has in its care 125 properties and 75,000 hectares (185,000 acres) of land.

To visit a National Trust property is to step into a piece of Britain's heritage. From Hill Top, birthplace of Peter Rabbit and other famous characters created by Beatrix Potter, to spectacular Tyntesfield in Somerset, from Lundy Island in the Bristol Channel to the Farne Islands, there is some part of the nation's history in the NT's devoted care.

TODAY
Beatrix Potter bequeathed Hill Top farm, near Sawry, to the National Trust, which keeps the farm house and its garden exactly as she left it.

1939
The talk among the patrons of this London pub is all about the War, a weighty matter best discussed over a pint and with one's pipe at full blast.

THE PUB

The character of the public house, licensed to sell beers and spirits to local people – mostly men – has changed fundamentally in recent decades. A change in drinking habits, begun when men chose to go to working men's clubs rather than to the pub, was accelerated by television, which has tended to keep families at home in the evenings.

There were some 50,500 pubs in the UK at the millennium, about 6 per cent fewer than in 1990. But pubs still have sales totalling nearly £14 billion in the UK, and many of them are radically changing what they offer in order to attract more customers.

The biggest change that publicans have made is to sell proper food, of an increasingly high standard. Pubs with a theme (Irish is very popular these days), pubs that offer karaoke or DJs on Friday and Saturday nights, quiz evenings and jazz nights all attract the crowds. But there's nothing like watching a big football match in a like-minded crowd, and football on the TV is getting people out of their living rooms and into the pub again.

TODAY

A big-screen TV, dropped down from the ceiling, allows the patrons of this pub to share all the joy and anguish of an England match.

1932

A St Bernard rests after having won eight awards at Crufts. Its owner has slipped off her show-ring shoes and is having a quiet smoke.

CRUFTS

The world's greatest dog show does not need a long name: everyone knows what Crufts is. The annual competition, the most important in the pedigree dog show year, is named after Charles Cruft, the general manager of James Spratt, a dog-biscuit manufacturing company.

In 1886, Mr Cruft organized a dog show, perhaps seeing it as a good way to promote his company's products. The competition he began has been held every year since then, apart from the war years and one or two others. The 100th Crufts Show was held in 2003, with more than 22,000 dogs from 177 different breeds taking part.

Crufts was a show solely for British dogs until anti-rabies laws were relaxed. Now dogs from abroad can take part, provided they have won qualifying events at home. Dogs compete in seven major classes for the title Supreme Champion, take part in obedience cases, and demonstrate their speed and agility in other events. Owners and handlers start young: children from up to 20 countries help to show and handle dogs at each show.

TODAY

A congratulatory kiss for Jilly, a Petit Basset Griffon Vendeen, after winning Reserve Best in Show at Crufts in the 2011 show, held in Birmingham.

THE CHANNEL

Until the steamship brought regular services and cheap fares to the business, crossing the Channel was a hazardous and unreliable business dependent on tide, wind and weather.

The steamship made crossing the Channel so much easier that increasing numbers of people, many of them led by travel pioneer Thomas Cook, found their way to Europe. The age of the motor car gave cross-Channel ferries a new problem, overcome by treating cars as freight to be hoisted aboard with the help of a crane. Then came the roll-on, roll-off ferry, revolutionizing the cross-Channel trip for both commercial and holiday traffic.

But nothing has revolutionized cross-Channel travel like the Channel Tunnel. First planned by a Frenchman in 1802, attempted in 1880 and finally realized in 1994, the Channel Tunnel is used by a drive-on, drive-off shuttle train service and by a high-speed passenger service, operated by British, French and Belgian railways. With London only three hours from Paris, no wonder nearly eight million people travel under the Channel every year.

1926
This family's 1925 Morris Oxford
14/28 motor car has towed them
and their caravan, plus tent and dogs,
to Eccles, near Manchester.

CARAVANING

It does not take a large car to tow a caravan, so the motor car opened up new vistas of enjoyable holidays for British people in the years after the First World War. Visits to the countryside or the seaside, with a place to stay already attached to the car, sounded irresistible, especially with the Automobile Association and, later, the Caravan Club able to offer advice and assistance.

British-made Austin and Morris tourers could get about country roads at 48 kilometres an hour (30 miles an hour) and were reliable enough to need only simple repairs that most motorists could do themselves. The caravans they towed were not spacious, but had primus stoves for cooking and offered good shelter from bad weather.

The modern trailer or motor caravan is a very different thing, the grandest offering all the comforts of a hotel. Parked on a good caravan site, the facilities of which could include a swimming pool and tennis courts as well as the more usual shops and laundry facilities, even the simplest caravan offers its owners the chance of a memorable holiday.

TODAY
Everyone, including the dog, is
enjoying the sun at a caravan site at
Onich, on the shores of Loch Linnhe
in the Scottish Highlands.

WOMEN GET THE VOTE

Although the move towards parliamentary democracy in Britain began in 1832, with the first Reform Act, by the end of the century women could still see no sign that they would ever be involved in the process.

Mrs Emmeline Pankhurst organized the Women's Social and Political Union in 1905 and led the fight, with increasing violence, for women's suffrage. One way the union drew attention to the cause by publishing a newspaper, *Votes for Women*, which carried articles by the principal figures in the campaign, including Mrs Pankhurst and Mrs Emmeline Pethick-Lawrence.

During the First World War, women did much of the work that men had done before August 1914. Their reward was the vote for women over the age of 30, used for the first time in the General Election of December 1918. Today, all women have the vote and can take a full part in the electoral process.

TODAY
Women manning a polling place in the grounds of a bowling club in Tullibardine, Perthshire, taken over for a Scottish election in 1999.

PLEASURE PIERS

'A good pier has long been regarded as an essential to a seaside town,' noted a Brighton guide book in the 1890s. In 1872, Eastbourne, just along the coast from Brighton, got a pier to add to its other amenities. It was designed by the engineer Eugenius Birch, one of the country's most prolific pier designers. In 1888, a pavilion and concert hall were added to the pier's amenities, which included an American bowling saloon, a rifle saloon with electric targets, and matinees in the concert hall.

Eastbourne Pier almost became a casualty of war in 1940, when the Army considered blowing it up to prevent it being used by German landing parties. In the end the Army simply removed a section of decking instead.

The pier was refurbished in 1996 and its Victorian splendour recreated, though many of its amenities, including a family amusement centre, nightclub and waterfront bar, are very much of the twenty-first century. Eastbourne pier, unlike Birch's West Pier in Brighton, wrecked in a storm followed by fire in 2003, is again a premier south coast attraction.

TODAY
Sunbathers relax in front of
Eastbourne's recently refurbished
pier. Later, they will be able to enjoy
the pier's evening attractions.

1926
A new-issue K2 telephone box in a London street. The K2, designed by Giles Gilbert Scott in 1921, was Britain's best-known phone kiosk.

THE TELEPHONE ON THE STREET

When the telephone, patented by Alexander Graham Bell in 1876, was first made available for public use, callers were connected via a telephone exchange. An automatic dialling system, first used in Britain in 1912, made communication by phone much easier.

The General Post Office made the new system available in the street via a standardized design telephone box, introduced in 1921 and complete with dial phone, a coin box for payment and telephone directories. Painted bright red and with a royal crown displayed above the door, the telephone box remained a prominent piece of street furniture until the end of the century.

Declining standards of public behaviour brought about the end of the red telephone kiosk. Vandalized, their telephone books defaced and coin boxes broken into, most kiosks have been replaced by phones with plastic hoods and slots for payment cards.

TODAY
A mobile phone, often also serving as a camera, in every handbag or trouser pocket has made the street telephone box a rare sight.

SPORTS & ENTERTAINMENT **3**

1948
The 100 metres final: Lloyd LaBeach
(no. 57) of Panama coming third,
with Alastair McCorquodale (no. 36)
of Great Britain just missing a medal
in fourth place.

THE OLYMPICS IN BRITAIN

Britain has been the host nation of the Olympic
Games three times since the games of ancient
Greece were revived in the modern world at the
end of the nineteenth century. London hosted the
IVth Olympiad in 1908. Some 1,500 competitors
from 19 nations took part, and association
football was included for the first time.

London's second hosting came in 1948, three
years after the end of the Second World War.
This time, 4,468 competitors (390 of them
women) from 59 nations competed in 136
events over 17 sports. Two 'firsts' of the 1948
Games: starting blocks appeared on the athletics
track, in races from 100 metres to 400 metres,
and events were shown on home television.

There would be no feeling of austerity about
Britain's third hosting of the Olympics in 2012, or
the Paralympics that followed them. Rather than
make do with existing facilities – Wembley
Stadium had been the main venue in 1948 – a
stylish new Olympic Park was built at Stratford in
east London, with some sports also sited outside
London so that more spectators could attend.

TODAY
Cyclists test the 56 kilometres (35
miles) of Siberian pine timber which
form the track of the 6,000-seat
velodrome built for 2012.

MOTOR RACING

Once motor cars became reliable at speed,
motor racing took off. The first races were
over roads for long periods of time that tested
the endurance of car and driver alike.

The world's first special motor course was
built at Brooklands, near Weybridge in Surrey,
in 1906–7. Here, on a specially banked circuit,
the Brooklands Automobile Racing Club and
other clubs held races, driving tests, speed
trials and long-distance races for sports cars
and pure racing cars up to 1939. Circuits built
after Brooklands included Donington Park,
Brand's Hatch and, after the Second World
War, Silverstone in Northamptonshire, which
is today the venue of the British Grand Prix.

The first Grand Prix race was held in
France in 1906, and by the 1930s, when Grand
Prix races had long been held on closed
circuits, pit work on the cars was becoming
a fine art.

Today's Grand-Prix racing car's pit team is a
miracle of speedy efficiency, with each member
as important an element in the car's success as
the army of designers, engineers, technicians
and drivers who built the car in the first place.

TODAY
The Ferrari team's Brazilian driver Felipe
Massa comes in for a pit stop during the
2011 British Formula One Grand Prix at
the Silverstone circuit.

1934

A young Arsenal fan exercises his lungs at the start of a London derby, Arsenal v. Tottenham Hotspur, at Highbury, Arsenal's home from 1913.

FOOTBALL

Association football is Britain's favourite team sport, played and watched by millions. It has inspired best-selling novels, television soap operas, movies, plays and musicals.

The game in the UK today is run by four separate football associations, all descended from the Football Association founded in England in 1863. The FA and the Football League, founded in 1888, were both the first organizations of their kind in the world.

When the FA was formed, it had just a dozen or so teams to deal with, most of which were made up of players who worked together, rather than living in the same town. London's Arsenal team, for instance, was made up of workers at the Woolwich Arsenal – hence their nickname, 'the Gunners'.

Today, 314 clubs are affiliated to the FA and about 42,000 clubs are affiliated to the regional or district associations. The Scottish FA has 78 full and associate clubs and nearly six thousand registered clubs under its jurisdiction. No longer just a sport, football is very big business indeed and success is vital for a major club's wellbeing.

TODAY

Celtic fans in full voice get their club's colours well to the fore at one of the Glasgow team's home games.

1898

The grandstands are full and gipsy caravans, tents and carts crowd the traditional fairground at Epsom for the running of the Derby.

DERBY DAY

The Derby, a race for three-year-old colts and fillies, is one of the classics of British flat racing. It was first run at Epsom, even then a 50-year-old race course, in 1780.

By early in Victoria's reign, the Derby had become more than just another race. It was a highlight of the English racing calendar and a popular day out for the masses, who were able to enjoy all the fun of the fair that took over Epsom Downs for the day. William Frith's *Derby Day*, painted in 1858, captured well the fun and excitement of the occasion.

The Derby lost something of its shine in the last decade or so of the twentieth century. The prize money was less than that offered in other races and fewer people took time off in mid-week to attend. Moving the Derby to a Saturday and increasing the prize money helped return the race to the status of a must-attend event. The hospitality boxes and tents are packed, double-decker buses offer great views for those who come in them and the champagne flows freely. Within a horse-shoe's throw of them all, the bookies win fortunes.

TODAY

Racing fans crowd Epsom Downs on Derby Day. The on-course bookies are ranged along the fence, ready to take the punters' money.

HENLEY REGATTA

A high point of the year for the sport of rowing in Britain is the Henley Royal Regatta. The oldest rowing regatta in Europe and the most famous in the world, the first Henley Regatta was held in 1839, ten years after the first Oxford and Cambridge Boat Race was rowed over the reach at Henley-on-Thames.

Throughout Victoria's reign, the Henley Regatta was a major attraction for rowers and a high point of the summer social scene. Rowing clubs, universities and schools, both the great public schools and schools from local riverside towns, sent teams to compete for the various trophies, the oldest of which – the Grand Challenge Cup, for eights – was rowed for at the first Henley Regatta.

Today the Regatta, long a major event in the international rowing calendar, has acquired added celebrity. It was at the Henley Regatta that the five-times Olympic Gold Medal winner Steve Redgrave honed the race-winning skills that, added to years of practice on the Thames, enabled him to become the most successful rower of all time.

1934

The goalkeeper retains his flat cap when making a save at the Manchester City v. Portsmouth FA Cup final at Wembley Stadium.

THE FA CUP

English football has its most glorious day of the year when the final of the FA (Football Association) Cup is played. It is the climax of a knock-out competition involving teams from all the football divisions – and involving, too, enough luck to ensure that it is not always the great teams from the Premier Division who reach the later stages and even the final.

The first FA Cup final was held in March 1872, when a crowd of about two thousand people saw Wanderers beat the Royal Engineers 1–0 at Kennington Oval. Fifteen clubs, including Queen's Park, Glasgow, entered the competition 'for a Challenge Cup open to all clubs belonging to the Football Association'.

Scotland having long had its own FA Cup, today's FA Cup final is an all-English affair. While the strength of, and therefore the main interest in, English football lies in the week-by-week programme of the Football League, the FA Cup knock-out competition retains all its exciting magic, especially with the later rounds restored to its traditional ground, the hallowed turf of Wembley Stadium.

TODAY

The FA Cup is hoisted aloft by triumphant Manchester City players as they celebrate winning it in 2011.

1930

Highland Games rules require competitors tossing the weight to wear the kilt. This man has put on shorts beneath his kilt.

HIGHLAND GAMES

The athletics meetings known as Highland Games were first held in the highlands of Scotland early in the nineteenth century.

Similar sports meetings begun at much the same time, such as those in the Scottish lowlands (Border Games) and the Lake District of England (Lakeland Games), have lost something of their former glory. But the Highland Gathering, held every September at the small Deeside town of Braemar, continues to be very popular. The Queen and other members of the Royal Family never miss attending the Braemar Gathering if they are in residence at Balmoral Castle, the royal home in Scotland, just ten kilometres (six miles) away.

Most Highland Games are a mixture of standard track and field events and competitions with a more cultural flavour, such as Scottish country dancing and bagpipe playing. Some peculiarly Scottish events, like tossing the caber and tossing the weight, add to visitors' enjoyment.

TODAY

A competitor attempts to toss the caber – a tree trunk of unspecified size – at the Cowal Highland Gathering in Dunoon, Argyll.

77

Elegantly dressed Ascot race-goers make their way past ordinary folk who have no need of expensive grandstand tickets to enjoy their day.

ROYAL ASCOT

Queen Anne started the Royal Ascot race meeting at her racecourse near Ascot in 1711. The racecourse, which is near Windsor Castle, is one of the finest in the country and remains in royal hands. So does the organization of the Royal Ascot meeting, a highlight of the flat-racing season, which takes place in June.

Royal Ascot is today, as it has been since Edward VII's reign, the highest point of England's social whirl. It is the Queen's racecourse and the only one in the country where she and her family and other guests arrive by way of a drive in elegant horse-drawn carriages up the race track.

The quality of the racing is generally outstanding, too. It is flat racing, under Jockey Club rules, and the cream of the country's race horses are entered for the four days of racing. Among the most important of the races held during Royal Ascot week is the Ascot Gold Cup, a race over 4,023 metres (2½ miles) first run in 1807 and now the highlight of Ladies' Day, when women race-goes put on their largest and most extravagant hats.

TODAY

Ladies' Day at Royal Ascot, when the women's hats steal the limelight. Men, in contrast, wear grey toppers and morning coats.

1930s
A 1933 Crossley 10hp, entry no. 95,
splashes through a stream in rough
country during a 1930s staging of
the Scottish Rally.

CAR RALLYING

In the early days of car rallying, a sport that
included the excitement of driving cars across
country in all weathers, the sport was open to
everyone. A well-maintained and highly tuned
car was the key to success, and even a humble
Austin, Morris, Wolseley or Ford could provide
a triumphant win in a major event.

As engines became more sophisticated, with
electronic controls to increase efficiency and
improve performance, keen motorists wanting
to take part in the top rallies had to become
technically expert too.

Car rallying is a motor sport that everyone
with an ordinary car can enjoy, at the level of
car club and similar rallies, anyway. At the top
level of rallying – such as the Rally of Great
Britain, an event in the World Rally
Championship in which Britons have excelled
in recent years – cars must be highly tuned
and their drivers very skilled. The numbers
who turn out to watch, in snowy Scottish
forests and rain-swept Welsh hill country,
attest to the great attraction of a motor sport
with which all car drivers can identify.

TODAY
Mark Higgins of Great Britain in
action during the 2002 Network Q
Rally of Great Britain, held at
Margam Park, Cardiff, Wales.

CRICKET

The quintessentially English game of cricket, a
form of which had been played in England and
other countries for centuries, began in its
modern form in the peaceful village of
Hambledon in Hampshire in the 1760s.
Although much has happened to cricket since,
quiet cricket on village greens and in parks
remains the bedrock of the game.

The centre of the game had moved to
London by the 1790s, when the Marylebone
Cricket Club was formed. The rules of the
game were agreed at the MCC in 1835, and
have changed little in essentials since. Overarm
bowling was allowed after 1864 and the
classification of cricketers into Gentlemen and
Players (with their own dressing rooms at test
matches) was abolished in 1963.

Cricket is a hierarchy of club cricket, county
cricket, one-day cricket and test-match cricket.
The last is played between countries
introduced to the game by Victorian empire-
builders sent out to reproduce the English way
of life in their colonial possessions. For many,
cricket is the best legacy of the Empire.

TODAY
A giant TV screen displays the Lord's
website name during a test match
between England and Sri Lanka at
Lord's in 2002.

1956

John Lennon and the Quarrymen provide the music, complete with a tea-chest-and-broom-handle bass, at St Peter's Church fete, Woolton.

POPULAR MUSIC

A popular-music revolution got under way in Britain in the 1950s, strongly influenced by the amazing sounds coming across the Atlantic from such pioneers of rock 'n' roll as Bill Haley, Elvis Presley and Chuck Berry.

Skiffle was an early musical response in Britain to all this, and many teenagers formed their own skiffle groups. Few of them became as famous as John Lennon, whose first group, the Quarrymen, were happy to cut their performing teeth at church fetes and to include in their band a bass made out of a tea-chest, a broom handle and a length of string.

Today, great rock musicians are more likely to be found performing before vast crowds at yet another venue on their latest world tour or in front of equally large and often rain-soaked, mud-caked crowds at music festivals. Kicking off on the Isle of Wight in 1970 and at Glastonbury shortly afterward, the star-studded rock-music festival is now an essential part of the British summer scene. Festivals may be simply a case of sex, drugs and rock 'n' roll to their elders, but to the young they are musical heaven.

TODAY

The Reading Festival, one of the country's biggest rock-music events, gets underway again at Reading in Royal Berkshire.

1907
A throw-in is taken during a rugby game played at the Queen's Club, now better know for its tennis, in west London.

RUGBY

Rugby football gets its name from Rugby School in England, where it is claimed that in 1823 a boy first picked up the ball in a football game and ran with it. Until mid-century, football, as played in most English boys' public and grammar schools, was seen as one game, with variations. Eventually, the differences became annoying, and separate sets of rules were formulated for football and rugby, which itself later divided in union and league forms.

Rugby, taken to the far corners of the world by young empire-builders from English schools, is more limited in its international appeal than the much less physically violent football. Commonwealth countries such as Australia, New Zealand – home of the fearsome All Blacks – and South Africa provide particularly strong competition for the four home rugby union teams, with Argentina, France, Italy and others adding spice to the international game.

Both union and league rugby are strong sports in Britain today, played by hundreds of men (and rather fewer women) in both amateur and professional competitions.

TODAY
England's James Haskell is held by Joe Ansbro (Scotland) during the RBS Six Nations match at Twickenham, west London, in 2011.

Competitors in the marathon in the 1908 Olympics, held in London, are applauded as they run through a town on the race's Windsor–London route.

MARATHON RUNNING

The marathon is the longest race to figure in major athletics championships. It gets its name from the story of Phidippides, a Greek soldier who ran from the Battle of Marathon to Athens, 35 kilometres (22 miles) away, with the news of the Greeks' victory over the Persians.

When the first Olympic Games of the modern era were held in 1896, a marathon race was included. Set at 42 kilometres (26 miles), it had an extra 352 metres (385 yards) added in 1908 so that the competitors, having run from Windsor to London, would end up opposite the Royal Box in the White City stadium.

Today, Londonders can watch a great marathon every year. The London Marathon, first organized by Olympic Gold Medal winner Chris Brasher in 1981, is the world's biggest marathon. It draws the cream of the world's long-distance runners, plus thousands of amateurs running for personal satisfaction and to raise money for good causes.

TODAY

Competitors mingle with officials and spectators in The Mall after crossing the finishing line of the Virgin London Marathon in 2011.

GOLF

The modern game of golf developed in Scotland in the eighteenth century out of a game the Scots had played for centuries. Mary, Queen of Scots, was a keen payer and her son, James VI (James I of England), took the game to England, although it did not really catch on south of the border until late in the nineteenth century.

Golfers from a new club at St Andrews in Scotland, later the Royal and Ancient Golf Club of St Andrews, administer the rules of golf worldwide, except in the USA and Mexico. The rules they administer are infinitely more complex than the 13 they started with in 1754.

Golfers have a choice of more than two thousand courses on which to play the game in the UK today. The amateur game long ago opened its doors to women, whose golf is governed by the Ladies' Golf Union. For every lover of the game, the highlight of the golfing year is the Open Championship, one of the world's four 'major' events.

TODAY
Northern Ireland golfer Darren Clarke holds aloft the famous Claret Jug after winning the Open, Britain's premier golf championship, in 2011.

1955
A state occasion at Covent Garden. The Queen, the President of Portugal and their suites arrive for a performance of *The Bartered Bride*.

OPERA FOR ALL

There has been an opera house in London's Covent Garden since 1732, and the present building is the third one on the site. Until World War II it was privately owned and presented seasons of opera and ballet to largely rich and aristocratic audiences.

After 1945, when the Royal Opera House re-opened as a public company and was given a state subsidy, its audiences changed, in line with the social changes that were taking place in Britain. Black tie and evening dress, essential in 1946, had given way to jeans and T-shirts (in the stalls as well as the gallery) by 1997, when the Opera House closed for a controversial and very expensive refit.

In its handsomely rebuilt and much more welcoming new form, the Royal Opera House is still devoted to its core ideal of presenting opera and ballet to world-class standards. But this is an expensive business and publicly funded organizations must not seem elitist. A giant screen in the Piazza is one of several ways in which the Royal Opera House makes its productions more accessible to everyone.

TODAY
Hearing Placido Domingo for free. A performance in the Royal Opera House is shown in the Covent Garden Piazza.

1960
Racing yachts in action off the Isle of Wight during the annual Cowes Week regatta.

SAILING

The British, called 'an island race' so often it is almost a cliché, nevertheless have a special relationship with the sea. The poet John Masefield called it 'sea fever', and wrote that 'the call of the running tide … is a clear call that may not be denied'.

At the 2000 Olympic Games, the British team demonstrated this special relationship by winning five medals, making Britain the most successful nation in the sailing events.

Where 'sailing' once meant simply being at sea in a craft with a sail, today it is a broad term covering yacht and dinghy sailing, powerboat racing, motor cruising, jet skiing and windsurfing on inland and offshore waters. One of the main aims of sailing's national body, the Royal Yachting Association, is to make all forms of boating as accessible as possible.

From club moorings and harbour jetties, from river mouths, beaches and rocky shores all round the coast, nearly eight million men and women launch themselves on to waters in and around Britain every year in pursuit of their favourite form of sailing.

TODAY
Spinnakers billow as yachts return from a day's racing at Cowes. Every British sailor's dream is to take part in a race during Cowes Week.

1921

The Nottingham Goose Fair is in full
swing, and the crowds enjoy the
wide range of attractions and
entertainments on offer.

FUN AT THE FAIR

Many of the fairs held round the United
Kingdom every year are descendants of the
great markets and fairs that were established
by royal charter from medieval times for the
sale of a wide range of foods and goods or for
the hiring of labour. Some can trace their
beginnings to Saxon times.

Nottingham's Goose Fair, three days of fun
and merrymaking every October, was
established by a charter of Edward I as an
annual fair for the selling of geese and other
goods. Thousands of geese were driven to the
fair, their feet treated with tar and sand to help
them cover the many miles from as far away as
Lincolnshire and Norfolk.

Geese ceased to be the major reason for
the Nottingham Goose Fair long ago and by
the nineteenth century people were going to it
just for the merrymaking. Today, Goose Fair is
a national institution, and one of the biggest
annual funfairs in the country. Its opening is
proclaimed by the town clerk with full
traditional ceremony, involving the Lord Mayor
and the Sheriff of Nottingham.

TODAY

A brilliantly lit helter-skelter
dominates the Nottingham Goose
Fair, still one of the great attractions
in the Midlands every year.

COUNTRY LIFE 4

c.1914
Target shooting practice with a
difference. Three men and a dog in a
boat, rat shooting on the Norfolk
Broads.

FIELD SPORTS

Field sports in the UK include hunting,
shooting, stalking, ferreting, falconry and hare
coursing. Country people have followed them
all for centuries, in the past more for survival
than for sport. Today, shooting is the favourite
field sport for thousands of men and women
in all parts of the country.

Not all shooting is for live birds or game.
Clay pigeon, or trap, shooting, and skeet, which
grew out of sportsmen's desire to have all-
year-round shooting practice, quickly became
very popular sports in their own right. Clay-
shooting schools are increasing in number all
over the UK.

Game-bird shooting seasons are strictly
controlled in the UK, to protect bird
populations and their breeding seasons. The
grouse shooting season, for instance, starts on
August 12, long known as 'the Glorious
Twelfth'. From then until early December, butts
on the grouse moors of Scotland are filled
with sportsmen and women seeking, often at
considerable expense, to shoot hundreds of
birds a day.

TODAY
Enjoying the start of the grouse
shooting season from a butt on the
Moy Estate near Inverness in
Scotland.

c.1900

The cattle section of the centuries-old charter market on Gloucester Green, in the heart of Oxford, in full swing.

MARKET DAYS

For centuries, livestock and food markets in towns and villages were the main outlets for farmers' cattle and produce. Market day might have been a day for doing business, but it was also a social occasion, and a time for meeting friends over pints of ale in the market tavern.

Changing trading patterns and transport systems, and more stringent health laws, caused livestock markets to be merged on sites away from town centres. While general markets still flourish, most of us today buy our food at supermarkets, where much of what is on the fresh food shelves gets there long after it leaves the farm it was grown on.

To meet the growing demand for fresh, organically grown food, farmers have started bringing their own food to town again. Farmers' markets have become the only place in town, from Islington and Pimlico in London to Aberystwyth and Hexham, for buying fresh meat, fruit and vegetables, unpasteurized cheeses, venison sausages and a lot more. There is even a fully-fledged National Association of Farmers' Markets to oversee their work.

TODAY

The stalls at the farmers' market at Blackheath, in south London, are manned by growers who bring their own produce to market.

COUNTRY CRAFTS

Although farming in Britain is a highly mechanized business, many old crafts and skills, once essential to maintaining a farm's land and buildings in good condition, are still practised today. Some, like thatching and hedge-laying, are no longer vitally important in modern countryside management but are kept going by organizations such as the Countryside Agency because they provide such strong links with the country's past.

Other crafts are still a part of everyday life in many parts of Britain. Go to County Armagh in Northern Ireland or to Sutherland and Strathspey in the far north of Scotland and you will find people cutting precisely sized turfs from the peat bogs for winter fuel.

In Welsh slate quarries, slate is split and prepared to make roofing tiles. And in many upland districts of Britain, such as the Derbyshire Peak District and the Yorkshire Moors, stone from the land provides material for drystone walls that shelter stock and withstand for decades the wind and weather that would rapidly destroy hedges and fences.

TODAY
A splendid vista of drystone walls marking field boundaries in the Derbyshire Peak District.

NATIONAL PARKS

The idea of establishing national parks in Britain grew out of a fear that too much of the countryside was being lost to industry and the spread of urbanization and, at the same time, that too few people were able to enjoy the beauty of Britain's lovely land. National parks, established by an act of parliament in 1949, are areas of countryside where the landscape, biodiversity and recreational resources are recognized as having national importance.

The country's first national park was the Peak District National Park, mainly in Derbyshire but extending into surrounding counties, which was established in 1951. It was soon followed by the Lake District National Park in Cumbria and the Snowdonia National Park, covering 2,180 square kilometres (838 square miles) of wild and beautiful country in Gwynedd, North Wales, with the Snowdon massif at its heart.

Today there are eight national parks in England, three in Wales and one in Scotland, each containing countryside of great natural beauty and extraordinarily diverse ranges of flora and fauna.

EQUESTRIAN EVENTS

The steam and combustion engines may have ended the horse's essential part in transport, but it still plays a major role in people's leisure activities, especially in the country.

The late nineteenth and early twentieth centuries saw a blossoming of many kinds of equestrian competition. Some of them, like point-to-points, involved races across country, and others, like show jumping, took place in show rings at agricultural shows. Between the wars, horse-riding and the many events associated with it flourished, with many Pony Clubs helping to train children to become the competitive riders of the future.

Competing with show-jumping in popularity today, among both competitors and spectators, is the Three-Day Event or Horse Trials. This supreme form of horse competition, held over three days, tests the all-round ability of horse and rider by way of dressage; speed, endurance and cross-country; and show jumping.

c.1930
Hounds lead the way as a hunt
moves off from its gathering place in
front of a Tudor house in the village
of Eynsford, Kent.

FOX HUNTING

Hunting has long been a traditional country
activity. Organized fox-hunting, which began in
the eighteenth century, soon became a regular
part of the winter scene, especially in those
Midlands counties such as Leicestershire
where the rolling fields and scattered pockets
of woodland made ideal hunting country.

Oscar Wilde may have crisply summarized
fox-hunting as 'the unspeakable in full pursuit
of the uneatable', but for most people riding to
hounds has meant being able to gallop across
country and face up to the challenges posed
by ditches, hedges, fences and stone walls.

Fox-hunting in modern Britain is not such a
carefree experience. Modern farming practice,
which involves knocking down fences and
grubbing out hedges to make room for giant
farm machinery, has radically altered much of
the rural landscape. Acts aimed at banning
hunting animals with dogs were passed in the
Scottish and English parliaments early in the
twenty-first century, but hunts flourished
nonetheless; in 2011, 300,000 people attended
Boxing Day meets throughout the country.

TODAY
The Avon Vale Hunt moves off from
a Boxing Day meet in Lacock,
Wiltshire in 2011.

1937
A team of four heavy horses
provides the power that pulls the
plough on a farm near Paddock
Wood in Kent.

HORSE POWER ON THE FARM

Handsome heavy horses once provided most
of the power needed to work farmland, pulling
ploughs, harrows and drills. They symbolized
the endless toil and ceaseless care that went
into creating the British farming landscape.

Heavy horses still work in Britain, often in
small, enclosed areas and woodland where
machinery is too large to use. But for most of
us, the only connection we have today with
these magnificent creatures is the horse
brasses from their collars and harness that
decorate the bars of country pubs or find
their way into antique and bric-a-brac shops.

When horse power came to mean the
power in the engines of farm machinery,
farming changed radically, especially in those
areas where crop-growing was paramount.
Fewer people now worked in agriculture, and
hundreds of miles of centuries-old hedgerows
were torn out to make large fields that the
great machinery could manoeuvre in.

TODAY
A mighty combine harvester and
tractor team up to move across a
large field and harvest its crop of
winter wheat.

CHURCH FETES

A conscientious Victorian vicar or rector and his wife, spending most if not all of their time in their country parish, could fill much of their day visiting the old, sick and disabled, overseeing and even teaching at the village's church school, or holding adult education classes in the vicarage.

In our own, more affluent times, the state has taken over many of these responsibilities and church-goers need be less concerned with the problems and needs of the poor at home than with those in third-world countries. For them, the country church remains a very active and often architecturally beautiful centre of Christian worship as well as a focal point of village social life.

Today, as in Victorian times, the rural church fete – with its beer and tea tent, home-made cake and embroidery stalls, bran tub for the children and games for everyone – remains a high point in the local social calendar, as well as an important source of funds for the upkeep of the church.

TODAY
The vicarage garden at the Anglican church in Boxford, Suffolk, is large enough to hold a big tent and the stalls for the annual church fete.

115

c.1930

Only a cyclist breaks the stillness of the day in front of the Greyhound Hotel, once a less grand-sounding inn, in Corfe, Dorset.

STAYING IN THE COUNTRY

The railway and the motor car changed the city dweller's attitude to the country. While the Edwardian upper classes perfected the art of the country-house weekend, everyone else who had a car or a motorcycle began to discover the delights of country inns, hitherto used to provide a night's food and a bed for relatively few coach travellers.

Country inns, often simple places, were soon upgrading their facilities and putting in extra bathrooms and lavatories. Others joined in the business, so that offering 'bed and breakfast' became a valuable source of extra income for many in country villages and on farms.

Today, the country holiday, promoted by tourist authorities and local councils, can mean bed and breakfast in a country pub, self-catering in a remote farm cottage, or being pampered in a luxurious country-house hotel. They all make great holidays and are invaluable revenue earners for the countryside.

TODAY

Time for a chat outside the George Inn at Bathampton, near Bath, where sawn-off lengths of tree trunk provide the drinks tables.

CHANGING CITY 5

WESTMINSTER ABBEY

Among the many features that attract visitors to the Gothic splendour of near-1,000-year-old Westminster Abbey in London, few arouse as much emotional response as the Grave of the Unknown Warrior. Set under a black granite slab in the floor of the nave near the Abbey's great West Door, it contains the body of a British serviceman, 'unknown by name or rank', killed on the Western Front during World War I.

Brought with some ceremony from France, the body was interred in the Abbey on 11 November 1920 to commemorate 'the many multitudes who during the Great War of 1914–1918 gave the most that Man can give – life itself – for King and Country'.

In 1923, Lady Elizabeth Bowes-Lyon married the Duke of York, later King George VI, in Westminster Abbey. After the ceremony, she sent her bouquet to be placed on the grave in memory of her young brother, Fergus, killed on the Western Front in 1915.

Her action began a tradition for royal brides married in Westminster Abbey. In April 2011, the new Duchess of Cambridge followed suit with her bouquet of delicate white blooms.

1925
Another great ship, RMS *Asturias*,
leaves the slipway after its launch at
Belfast docks on 7 July.

BELFAST

Back in the nineteenth century, Belfast was
one of the fastest-growing cities in the British
Isles as it developed its ship-building and
engineering industries. At the huge Harland
and Wolff Shipyard many of the world's great
liners, including the White Star Line's *Titanic*,
were built and launched.

The development of the jet engine, which
made long-haul flights possible, meant the end
of the great days of the ocean liner and also
severely damaged merchant shipping. Belfast's
glory days were over, the dockyard cranes no
longer dominated Belfast's waterfront skyline,
and shipyards closed. After this disaster,
Northern Ireland also endured terrible years
of virtual civil war that polarized society.

There is a new spirit abroad in Belfast today,
and an optimism that is everywhere expressed
in a large rebuilding programme. One of the
finest of the new buildings in Belfast is the
Waterfront Hall, described as 'a fresh,
Modernist take on the Albert Hall', the curved
glass frontage of which is very different to the
cranes that once lined the waterfront.

TODAY
Concert-goers at Belfast's splendid
Waterfront Hall, opened in 1997,
have a fine view of the River Lagan
from the hall's entrance foyers.

It is a hot, sunny day in Preston, Lancashire, and the shops along Fishergate have drawn their awnings down over their windows.

ENGLAND'S NEWEST CITY

There are 66 urban areas in the United Kingdom – 50 of them in England, six in Scotland, five in Wales and five in Northern Ireland – that have been granted city status, a great mark of distinction.

Although a town may think it has all the attributes of a city, only the sovereign, on the advice of her ministers, can grant city status.

Three towns, Brighton & Hove and Wolverhampton in England and Inverness in Scotland, were granted city status in 2000 to mark the millennium.

England's latest city is Preston, a busy industrial and university city in Lancashire, famed in the nineteenth century for its cotton mills. Preston was one of five UK towns granted city status in 2002, to mark the Queen's Golden Jubilee. Competition for the honour was keen, but nobody denied that Preston, birthplace of Richard Arkwright who invented the spinning jenny, was a worthy recipient of it.

TODAY

A forest of poles and shop signs has replaced the awnings on the shops along Preston's busy Fishergate, still the city's main shopping centre.

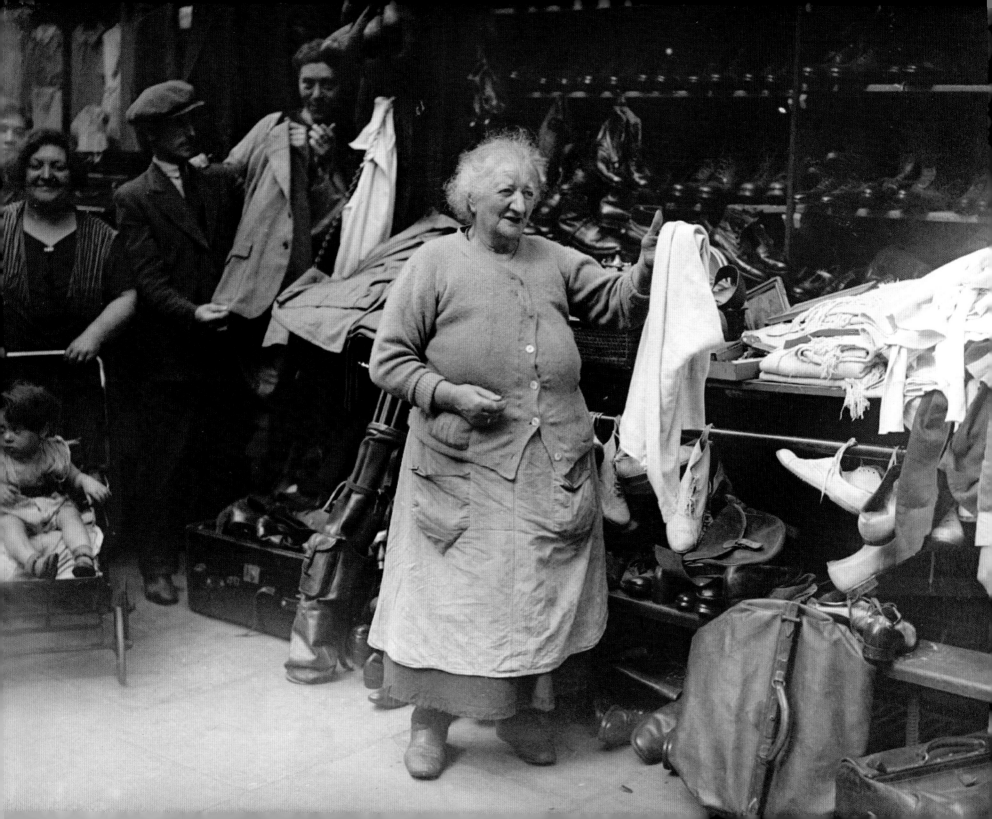

1930s
A second-hand clothes stall in Whitechapel, the Jewish quarter of London's East End, where much trading was done on the streets.

LONDON MARKETS

Shopping at market stalls in the street was the norm in the poor districts of London from the nineteenth century up to World War II. Cheap food and clothing were the most essential goods for the low-paid workers who crowded into the run-down housing near the markets. Much of this housing was medieval in origin, while other areas grew up to feed the needs of immigrant populations fleeing persecution, such as the Huguenots and Jews.

The changing ethnic mix of London's population has changed the character, but not the liveliness and vibrancy, of London's street markets. Brick Lane, in Shoreditch, began as a fruit and vegetable market in the eighteenth century and now has many Asian stallholders and shoppers. Brixton, in south London, is the place to go to find the fruits and vegetables essential for good West Indian cooking. And Petticoat Lane, its Sunday opening indicating its Jewish origins, offers something for everyone.

TODAY
Clothes are still a big draw at Petticoat Lane Market, crowded every Sunday with shoppers of many ethnic groups.

1941

Fire-watchers on the roof saved St Paul's Cathedral from the consequences of the bombs that destroyed much of the City of London in World War II.

ST PAUL'S IN WAR & PEACE

Every great city needs a focus for its pride and self-belief. Sir Christopher Wren's great masterpiece in the City of London, St Paul's Cathedral, provides such a focus for Londoners. St Paul's was built after the Great Fire of London destroyed the old cathedral in 1666. Nearly three hundred years later, the cathedral survived a far more devastating series of fires, the result of the Blitz of the Second World War.

In 1941, pictures of the dome of St Paul's rising undamaged through the smoke and fire of the Blitz did almost as much as Winston Churchill's stirring speeches to maintain morale and confidence on the Home Front.

St Paul's remains a focus of national pride, most recently during the celebrations for Elizabeth II's Golden Jubilee. An exciting new view of the dome and south side of St Paul's was opened up for Londoners when a pedestrian walk was constructed down to the new Millenium footbridge over the Thames to the South Bank.

TODAY

Unchanged in the midst of change, the great dome of St Paul's Cathedral rises above surrounding buildings and the streams of traffic.

1937

The Muslim community in Wales forms a procession through the streets of Cardiff as part of the El Elbekir religious ceremony.

THE CHANGING ETHNIC MIX

Perhaps because its early history involved the settling on its lands of so many culturally diverse peoples, Britain has always given a sympathetic, if sometimes muted, welcome to outsiders coming in search of a better life.

Whether they have been Huguenots fleeing from religious persecution in France, Jews escaping the horrors of Nazi Germany, or men and women from many of Britain's former imperial possessions, most immigrants have chosen to live in big cities. This has given many British cities an extraordinarily vibrant cultural and ethnic diversity.

Among the longest-term 'newcomers' are Muslim people. There has been a Muslim community in Britain since the sixteenth century and today their faith, Islam, is the most common in Britain after Christianity. More than a third of British Muslims live in London and many more live in the cities of the West Midlands. Their community in Wales, mostly in Cardiff, is much smaller.

TODAY

A British-Yemeni boy is given instruction on the finer points of the Qur'an at the South Wales Islamic Centre mosque in Cardiff.

131

TRANSPORT IN THE CITY

Because the early railway was not ideal for urban transport, the first mass moving of people round towns and cities was by double-decker, horse-drawn omnibus.

The first omnibus route in London opened in 1829 and by the 1860s omnibuses were carrying 40 million passengers a year. Other big cities could boast similar numbers. By the end of the century horse-drawn omnibuses were being replaced by petrol-driven ones.

Urban railways went underground in 1863, with the construction of the Metropolitan Line in London, and two decades later urban tramways turned electric, the first electric trams running in Blackpool in 1885.

Trams and light railways, which do not generate as much pollution as buses, are back in fashion in Britain's cities today. The 1990s saw tram and light-railway systems opening across the country, in London's Docklands and Croydon as well as Birmingham, Manchester and Newcastle.

TODAY
Manchester's Metrolink, officially opened in 1992, is Britain's first modern street-operating light-rail system.

c.1900

Sailing ships and steam freighters are moored closely together in the crowded West India Docks on the Thames in East London.

LONDON'S DOCKLANDS

Until the advent of World War II, the Thames below London Bridge was always crowded with ships from Britain's worldwide empire unloading their goods. Ships that could not find a berth on the river were moved into specially built docks, known by their trading regions – such as the West India Docks and the East India Docks – or given royal names.

London's docklands was a very picturesque quarter, the masts and riggings of the ships and the dockside cranes providing a backdrop for an area teeming with cosmopolitan life. Chinatown had the best Chinese restaurants in England – and the most opium dens.

A thriving new city, still called Docklands, has taken over the docks today. Towering office buildings rise above smart riverside housing, pubs, stylish restaurants and shops. In the old docks, cabin cruisers, sailing boats and floating restaurants bob on the waters once filled with the shipping of a great empire.

TODAY

At Canary Wharf, towering office blocks displaying the names of major banks reveal Docklands as a modern financial hub.

1858
The towers of York Minster loom over carriages in the sidings at York railway station, built just inside the ancient walls of the city.

HISTORIC YORK

Ironically – given its present troubles with flooding, supposedly caused by global warming – the Romans chose York as a site for its fortress of Eburacum because it was very dry.

After the Romans came the Danes, who founded a colony here, then the Normans, who built massive fortifications of their own, including great walls, partly on Roman foundations. Real prosperity came to York with the medieval wool trade, much of the profits of which went – over two and a half centuries – into the building of York's magnificent Minster, seat of the Archbishop of York, which has been called a 'poem in stone'.

Today, York within its city walls is virtually, as King George VI once remarked, a living museum of English history from Roman times, via the Danes – the Jorvic Centre, about Viking life, is a big draw – to the present day. Its Castle Museum and Heritage Centre are other attractions that help bring thousands of visitors to York every year. Outside the medieval walls, York is home to the National Railway Museum.

TODAY
Flowerbeds give splashes of colour to the lawns beneath York's city walls. Only the trappings of traffic control hint that this is present-day York.

ARCHITECTURE AND THE CITY

In the 1960s, Birmingham's Bull Ring became a prime example of what can go wrong when city planners decide to bulldoze the old centres of their cities and recreate them in 'modern' style.

Many British cities had huge problems of urban rebuilding and regeneration after World War II. But in too many of them, the arrival of the bulldozer meant the replacing of old city centres and domestic housing with concrete high-rise architecture so stark and so riddled with wind tunnels and exposed walkways that 'brutalism' seemed an apt name for it indeed.

In the 1990s, Birmingham, already brimming with the cultural self-confidence of a city possessing a major symphony orchestra, a leading ballet company and a superb exhibition centre, embarked on a modernization programme that is restoring it to its place as one of Britain's finest cities. The city's current £6 billion ten-year redevelopment plan for its East Side includes a gleaming new public library.

TODAY

This aerial view of the heart of Birmingham, round the Bull Ring, shows the scale of the rebuilding being undertaken there.

1928

George Stephenson designed Newcastle's great two-tier Tyne Bridge, which was opened in 1849. The bridge carries a railway line and a road over the River Tyne.

TYNESIDERS

The River Tyne in the north-east of England separates two great metropolitan areas. Newcastle upon Tyne, a cathedral and university city on the river's north bank, is a major ship-building and marine-engineering centre. Gateshead, on the south side of the river, is a rapidly growing cultural, sporting and shopping centre for the region.

The two are working together to spearhead the regeneration of the Tyneside region, with a large investment in culture. Although Newcastle-Gateshead did not succeed in its bid to be the British candidate for the title of European Capital of Culture in 2008, the attempt helped to revitalize the region. 'Newcastle-Gateshead Buzzin' was the image projected for the bid.

Today there is plenty buzzing along the Tyne to support the image, from the BALTIC Centre for Contemporary Arts on the Tyne in Gateshead to the amazing Millennium Bridge, assembled at a Tyneside shipyard and lifted into position over the river by one of the world's largest floating cranes.

TODAY

The Gateshead Millennium Bridge, completed in 2001, is the world's first rotating bridge and opens in a 'blinking eye' movement.

1953
It's Saturday night in Glasgow and
crowds throng the intersection of
Hope Street and Sauchiehall Street
in the centre of the city.

GLASGOW

The great Scottish comedian Harry Lauder
used to sing about Glasgow belonging to him,
rather than he to the city, after a drink or two
on a Saturday night. That was when Glasgow,
Scotland's second city, still had a great ship-
building industry along the River Clyde and the
prosperity that went with it.

The destruction of large parts of the Clyde
ship-building docks during World War II,
followed by the collapse of the ship-building
industry, meant that Glasgow had to pick itself
up, dust itself down and start all over again.

Glasgow's appointment as European City of
Culture in 1990 spurred the city on to greater
efforts to revitalize its flagging economy. In the
1990s the city replaced its almost vanished
imperial-age industries with something very
different: culture and shopping. Glasgow today
has a vibrant theatre life, a new Royal Concert
Hall, superb art galleries and a new Museum of
Education. These, and the fact that Glasgow is
now Britain's second-biggest shopping city,
attract thousands of visitors. Harry Lauder
would be proud to belong to Glasgow today.

TODAY
Outwardly not much changed,
Glasgow's Hope Street/Sauchiehall
Street crossroads is today part of
Britain's second-biggest shopping city.

EVERYDAY LIVING 6

OVER THE SEA TO SKYE

The beautiful, mountainous Isle of Skye, off the west coast of Scotland, is celebrated for its place in the story of Bonnie Prince Charlie's escape from the disaster of Culloden in 1746. He made the hazardous journey disguised as Flora Macdonald's maid 'over the sea to Skye' from Benbecula, in the Outer Hebrides.

Had he gone from the mainland, there would have been no story, for the crossing is little more than a stone's throw. The narrow crossing from the Kyle of Lochalsh to Kyleakin on Skye was made by motor boat or car ferry until 1995, when a road bridge was opened.

The new, costly bridge was a toll bridge – much to the rage of local people, forced to pay the toll to get themselves, their sheep and their cattle to and from the mainland because the car ferry was withdrawn and other island services were summer-only. A long anti-toll campaign bore fruit in 2004, when the Skye Bridge tolls were abolished.

TODAY

The gracefully arched Skye Road Bridge, spanning the narrow sea crossing from the Scottish mainland to the Isle of Skye, opened in 1995.

1890
Morning church service over, the congregation in their Sunday best walk home to Sunday lunch down Brading High Street, Isle of Wight.

FLOURISHING CHRISTIANITY

Christianity has been the most important religion in the UK for fifteen centuries. It is the faith that the great majority of Britons – who may be Anglican, Catholic or nonconformist – put on passport and census forms, the latter for the first time in the 2001 census. There is a distinction to be made, however, between 'community size' and 'active membership' figures, and the number of people who actively follow a Christian life has been falling.

Christianity in Britain remains richly varied and diverse. People from many different cultures have migrated to Britain since the Middle Ages, bringing their kind of Christianity with them. Communities of Greek and Coptic Orthodox churches, Armenian, Lutheran and Reformed churches from all over Europe can be found in large cities such as London.

Outnumbering them are growing numbers of lively communities of charismatic and Pentecostal churches, boosted by immigration from the Caribbean since World War II.

TODAY
The choir in full voice at a packed session of the nonconformist Morris Cerullo Mission at Earl's Court in London.

THE RAILWAY AGE

Railways were pioneered in Britain early in the nineteenth century. The 1830 opening of the Liverpool to Manchester Line, which carried both people and goods, triggered a massive railway boom during which, while fortunes were made and lost, a great railway network was built. By 1912 it covered over 11,160 kilometres (18,000 miles) and brought most people in Britain within reasonable reach of a train.

Despite a wide-ranging closure of unprofitable lines in the 1960s, Britain still has 32,000 kilometres (20,000 miles) of railway track and 2,500 railway stations, even though many small ones were sold off, their tracks lifted and the station buildings converted to houses and offices.

Today, the railways are fighting back against the competition of road and air transport. Inter-city services have been speeded up and local services have been transformed by the introduction of light railways in and between cities. So far, there are five light railways in operation in England and more planned. Britain's railway age still has a long run ahead.

TODAY
The light-rail service the Docklands Light Railway connects London's Docklands with surrounding areas and the City of London.

Two begowned undergraduates of
Cambridge University discuss life
from the saddles of their 'sit-up-and-
beg' bicycles.

UNIVERSITIES

Educating good numbers of the country's young
to a high standard became important when
Britain became an industrialized society, which is
why so many technical colleges and places
offering practical advanced learning were
founded in Britain during the course of the
nineteenth century.

A university education remained something for
a minority of young people until well after the
Second World War, although the 1944 Education
Act, which established secondary education for
all, at least ensured plenty of potential students
from among those who obtained good results in
their final-school-year examinations.

University education began a great expansion in
the 1960s, with the founding of new universities –
including the Open University – and polytechnics
and the conversion of many other higher-
education foundations to full university status.

The State would like to see half the country's
young people undertaking some form of higher
education. This is an expensive ambition, and a
government decision that young people should
help pay for it, via a swingeing increase in
university fees from 2012, caused a major outcry.

TODAY
All that hard work at school has
paid off for this girl, waving the
A-level results that will get her into
university at her overjoyed mother.

153

It is the beginning of the Jewish new year 5698, and Jews gather at Tower Bridge to carry out the ceremony of casting their sins upon the waters.

OBSERVING THE SABBATH

The small Jewish community in England, well established by the eighteenth century and with its own synagogue in Aldgate, London, was greatly enlarged from the 1880s onwards by Jews fleeing persecution in Europe and Russia.

The largest communities of Jews in Britain were to be found in the East End of London, especially in Whitechapel, where their particular trade was tailoring. Jews were largely responsible for establishing the ready-made suits and clothing trade in Britain.

The Jewish community in Britain remains relatively small, coming fifth on the religion membership table, after Christians, Muslims, Hindus and Sikhs. Like other religions, Jews fall into separate groupings, Orthodox Jews being the most strict in their observance of religious laws. After many years' discussion, Orthodox Jews succeeded in 2003 in having an *eruv* marked out in Golders Green, London, within which they may relax their observance of some of the very strict laws governing their behaviour on the Sabbath.

TODAY

An Orthodox Jewish father and his child admire the poles and fine wire that mark out the 18-kilometre (11-mile) *eruv* set up in London in 2003.

1935
The No. 1 platform at Paddington
Station in the GWR's centenary year
is not much changed from the
platform that passengers used when
the station opened in 1854.

PADDINGTON & THE GWR

'God's Wonderful Railway' was how its
employees once described the Great Western
Railway. They probably meant not the deity but
the builder of the line from London to Bristol
– the great railway engineer, bridge builder and
ship builder Isambard Kingdom Brunel.

Brunel was appointed engineer of the Great
Western Railway in 1833, and between 1835
and 1841 built the GWR and all its tunnels,
bridges and viaducts. He designed its stations,
too, the most splendid of which was the
London terminal, Paddington Station.

Today, Paddington is a spruced-up, modern
railway terminus linked to Heathrow Airport
by a fast electric train service and providing
dozens of services a day to the west of
England and south Wales. From 2018, it will
also have a main central London station on
the high-frequency, high-capacity Crossrail
service running from Maidenhead and
Heathrow to the west of London to Shenfield
and Abbey Wood in the east.

TODAY
A multi-million-pound refurbishment
in the late 1990s revealed the glory
of Brunel's great glass-and-iron roof
at Paddington Station.

1926

Miners bringing up trucks of coal at the Cresswell Colliery, near Mansfield in Nottinghamshire, where coal mines were prosperous and modern.

FROM COAL TO OIL & GAS

From the reign of Elizabeth I to the reign of Elizabeth II, coal was a primary source of heat and power in Britain's homes, offices and factories. Today, it is not. It has been overtaken by other fossil fuels, oil and natural gas, much of which comes from the North Sea.

The North Sea oil and gas industries got into gear in the 1970s, at much the same time that coal mines were becoming unproductive and expensive to operate. A series of bitter strikes in the 1980s sounded the death knell of an industry that had been part of the nation's culture for centuries.

Today, the UK is the world's tenth-largest producer of crude oil and gas, and nearly three-quarters of the country's energy consumption is in the form of oil and natural gas. We still use a lot of coal, to make electricity and to have friendly open fires at home and in the pub, but it no longer provides work and a way of life for whole communities.

TODAY

On the drilling deck of the *Ben Reoch* oil rig in the East Brae field in the North Sea.

159

1908
A botany class in progress at a girls' school in London. The smock-clad girls are sitting at desks that would still be in use fifty years later.

EDUCATION

Primary education for all children became compulsory in Britain in the 1870s. Every town and village in the land had a school, many of them run by the different churches, where children were taught to read, write and do sums. For many years, boys and girls were separated, both in class and in the playground. They sat in bench-like desks set in neat lines facing their teacher and the blackboard.

In the days before radio, television and other distractions, many children filled their time out of school with occupations complementary to their school work. Children might collect and press the flowers they studied in botany, or put plant and flower cards, taken from their father's cigarette packs, into albums.

Primary-school teaching has become child-centred in mixed classes. Children are encouraged to be individuals, while working in groups. But some things do not change. The school playground is still a place where children can leap about and let off steam and many of the games they play were played by their grandparents at the turn of the century.

TODAY
Children playing hopscotch in the playground of a mixed primary school in Glasgow, Scotland.

QUEUING: A VERY BRITISH HABIT

Forming orderly queues to obtain anything
from stamps in the post office and tickets at
the cinema to a seat on a bus has long been a
sensible British habit. During the Second
World War it became almost a way of life as
shoppers queued in all weathers, ration books
at the ready, to buy permitted quantities of
many basic foods. Rationing, first imposed in
1940, did not end until 1953.

Queuing used to be a fine art, involving
careful decisions about which queue to join.
Except in the supermarket, that's no longer
necessary. Now, one queue usually snakes back
and forth across the available space, people
peeling off when a ticket window or counter is
free. The high point of the queuing year comes
with the January sales. Shoppers – Christmas
dinner hardly digested – take folding stools
and sleeping bags for an overnight wait, to be
the first through the doors on the opening day
of their favourite store's sale.

TODAY
Queuing, sometimes overnight, to
be first in the door at the January
sales is a fine British custom. Here,
Glasgow shoppers are lining up.

163

1946

A general view of 'Britain's £20,000 civilian aerodrome at Heath Row', nearing completion and intended to be the country's main air junction.

GETTING ABOUT BY AIR

When Britain's biggest 'aerodrome' fully opened near the small Middlesex village of Heath Row in 1948, tents and Nissen huts left over from the Second World War housed administration offices and passenger facilities.

The extraordinarily rapid growth in air travel within the UK and to destinations all round the world meant not only that Heathrow had to be enlarged again and again but also that many other airports had to be built – and enlarged – in all parts of the country.

Today, there are more than 150 licensed civil aerodromes in the UK, handling between them at the latest count over 181 million passengers a year and 2.3 million tonnes of freight. Heathrow is the world's busiest airport for international travellers, and Gatwick is the world's sixth-busiest. The tents and Nissen huts have long gone, of course, and today's big airports have shopping malls, cafés and multi-ethnic restaurants to ease the wait for flights.

TODAY

Moving walkways like this one at Manchester Airport help passengers make the long walk between terminal and departure gate.

1936

A Cornish housewife checks how a tray of pasties are getting on in her beautifully black-leaded coal-fired kitchen range.

KITCHENS

A heavy closed range, made of cast-iron and fired by wood or coal, became the main feature of kitchens during the Victorian era. Food was cooked in it, water was heated on it, and clothes were dried round it. It also kept the kitchen – and the whole house, if small – warm and snug.

The harnessing of gas and electricity as a cooking fuel changed everything. Closed ranges, which had once seemed the ultimate in convenience compared with open fires, were now torn out of kitchens in town and country. They were replaced by gas and electric cookers or, especially in country kitchens, by efficient new ranges, fired by gas, oil or electricity and with electric thermostats.

The modern kitchen is seldom the heart of the household, that role having been taken by the living room and the television. For many, the kitchen is either the place for quickly heating ready-prepared meals or a sort of space-age laboratory where the many highways and by-ways of gastronomy can be explored by people able to buy the ingredients of all the world's cuisines at the supermarket.

TODAY

This very stylish modern kitchen, essential utensils and cookbooks ready to hand, has its gas cooking hob separate from the oven.

1956
The first Hindu wedding to take place at India House, the office of the India High Commission in London, nears completion.

HINDUS IN BRITAIN

Most of the members of the Hindu community in Britain today originate from India, once the 'jewel in the crown' of the British Empire, though some Hindus have come from other former colonial territories, mostly in Africa, to which Indians migrated.

The first Indians to reach Britain came as servants of merchants returning home, having made their fortune in India. They were few in number and Indians, both Hindu and Muslim, were not seen in large numbers in Britain until they were encouraged to come to relieve the intense labour shortage after the Second World War.

Hindu communities are close-knit and their culture is important to them. London's Hindus demonstrated their devotion to Hindu culture and religion in the 1990s by raising within the community the money to build the magnificent Shri Swaminarayan Temple in London, the first purpose-built Hindu temple in Europe. Much of the marble for the temple was prepared and carved in India by master craftsmen and then transported to Britain.

TODAY
The building of the Shri Swaminarayan Hindu Temple in Neasden, North London, was paid for by the Hindu community.

1940

An unexploded bomb is no reason for not delivering the milk. To save precious fuel, the milkman uses horsepower to pull his milk float.

DELIVERING THE GOODS

The Victorians, with their railway lines reaching into all parts of the country, moved into the business of home deliveries with enthusiasm.

The post, milk, bread and newspapers were at the everyday end of a system that in time included huge mail-order catalogues from businesses such as the Army & Navy Stores, which offered to deliver everything from corsets to cricket pavilions to the ends of the Empire.

Even when war came to the Home Front in 1940, deliveries of essential goods still got through – both in town and country – however hazardous unexploded bombs made the job.

The home-delivery business flourishes in Britain, given new impetus by the Internet. People can sit at home and tick off on a screen the items on the weekly shopping list, sit back and wait to have them delivered to the front door, where the milkman, paper boy, postman and perhaps the local pizza restaurant will have already delivered their goods.

TODAY

A child helps her mother unload a delivery ordered from a supermarket by telephone or e-mail or via a website.

CELEBRATIONS 7

1953
Cardboard periscopes at the ready, huge crowds fill Trafalgar Square, ready to cheer Elizabeth II after her coronation on 2 June.

ROYAL JUBILEE

More than half a century ago, on 2 June 1953, the coronation of Elizabeth II brought crowds flocking into London from all over the country and the Commonwealth, eager for a glimpse of the young woman whose father's death a year earlier had made her queen. Many people had waited for days for the big event, and pouring rain did not dampen their enthusiasm.

Fifty years after that unexpected accession, London's streets were once again hung with banners and flags and were full of enthusiastic crowds, eager to celebrate with the Queen her fifty years on the throne.

The Queen and Prince Phillip drove to the service in St Paul's Cathedral in the same ornate gold coach that had taken her to her coronation. They came back up the crowd-filled Mall to watch an afternoon of parades and fun from the steps of the Victoria Memorial, then went to the balcony of Buckingham Palace to watch a unique 27-aircraft flypast. The atmosphere and excitement of the day showed that patriotism has not disappeared in an age of scepticism and doubt.

TODAY
Union flags flutter as the large crowd in The Mall watch the flypast that was part of the Golden Jubilee celebrations in 2002.

1956
The first stopping place for these new arrivals in England from the West Indies is the Customs Hall at Southampton docks.

NOTTING HILL CARNIVAL

Although many Britons grew rich on the West Indian sugar trade in the great days of Empire, few Caribbeans came to Britain.

Things changed after World War II, when a severe labour shortage in Britain led the government to promote the idea of finding work in Britain to people in the West Indies, where there was high unemployment. The first boatload of Jamaicans reached Britain in 1948. They were followed by thousands more and the UK's West Indian communities grew rapidly.

The Notting Hill Carnival began as a small, impromptu event among West Indians living in London's Notting Hill, notorious in the 1950s for its serious racial tensions. In 1965 a few of them brought their steel bands out into the street and began playing. Today, the Notting Hill Carnival is a colourful extravaganza of music, dancing and fantastic costume that brings hundreds of thousands of people of all races to Notting Hill to take part in the fun.

TODAY
The Notting Hill Carnival, an exuberant display of Caribbean culture, is the largest street carnival in Europe.

It is Burns Night: the haggis has been piped in and is about to be stabbed, doused in whisky and served with champit tatties and bashed neeps.

SCOTLAND CELEBRATES

The two greatest nights of celebration in Scotland's year come within weeks of each other in the depths of winter, when the glowing warmth provided by whisky, the Scots' national spirit, is very welcome.

Hogmanay, or New Year's Eve, is celebrated by many Scots at home, with visitors offered black bun and copious amounts of whisky. The ideal first visitor, or First Foot, of Hogmanay is dark-haired or carries a lump of coal to signify the wish that the home fire will burn brightly throughout the coming year. In Scotland's cities Hogmanay is an excuse for revelry all night among the crowds filling the streets.

On 25 January, Scots and non-Scots all over the world celebrate the birth of Robert Burns, the country's greatest poet. As well as reciting Robert Burns's poetry, the ceremony of Burns Night is centred on the haggis, a surprisingly tasty mixture of offal and oats, served with potatoes, swede and plenty of whisky.

TODAY

Hogmanay revellers enjoy the spectacular firework display above Edinburgh Castle, a highlight of New Year festivities in Scotland in 2011.

1920

The Cenotaph in Whitehall is surrounded by a silent crowd, many in uniform, marking the minute's silence at 11am on 11 November.

REMEMBRANCE SUNDAY

The guns of the First World War fell silent at 11am on 11 November 1918. Ever since, 11 November has been Armistice Day in Britain. For a week or so before, many people wear poppies in memory of the men who lost their lives in the poppy fields of Flanders and for those from the British Empire and Commonwealth who lost their lives in the many conflicts, large and small, that followed the Great War.

The anniversary of Armistice Day is marked in London by a wreath-laying service in Whitehall, around the Cenotaph designed by the architect Edwin Lutyens, which was unveiled on Armistice Day in 1920.

Some years ago, to avoid bringing London to a standstill on a weekday, the wreath-laying ceremony was moved to the Sunday nearest 11 November. Every year, on a Sunday morning in November, central London falls silent as the Queen leads the nation in remembering the men and women who died for their country.

TODAY

The Queen has seldom missed leading the nation in homage to its war dead, and she is the first to lay a wreath on the Cenotaph's steps.

CHINESE NEW YEAR

It is the tradition in China to visit relatives and distribute presents, symbols of goodwill and good fortune, at the start of the new year, which is given a new animal name according to a long-established 12-year cycle. These New Year traditions are celebrated in great style by Britain's Chinese population.

Communities of Chinese people developed in several of Britain's big cities in the twentieth century. Some set up restaurants or shops selling oriental foods and other goods that were becoming fashionable in Britain. Others came to work in the sweatshops of the clothing industry in the East End of London.

Chinese New Year is now celebrated every year, especially in London, and is enjoyed as much by British people and foreign visitors as by the Chinese themselves. London's Chinatown holds a huge and colourful parade, featuring beautiful models of dragons and performances of the lion dance, to enliven the wintry streets of Soho every January.

TODAY
London's Chinatown enjoys the parade that winds its way through Soho to mark Chinese New Year in 2002, the Year of the Horse.

GREAT LIFE EXPECTATIONS

In the early years of her reign, it was not an arduous task for Elizabeth II to send the by-now-traditional congratulatory telegram to those of her subjects in Britain and the Commonwealth who reached the notable age of 100. There were not too many of them. Today, there are a great many more, including, in 2000, the Queen's own mother.

Life expectancy rose greatly for men and women in the twentieth century. In 1901, the average life expectancy at birth for men was 48 years; by 2007 it had risen to 77.9. For women, the figures rose from 51.6 to 82 years.

Britons are living longer for many reasons. Rising standards of living, healthier eating habits and enormous advances in medicine and medical technology have helped adults survive much longer. Perhaps 100 will come to seem so commonplace a birthday that Elizabeth II's successors will stop sending congratulatory telegrams to those subjects who reach it.

TODAY
The royal coat of arms on its cover announces that the telegram this 100-year-old lady is holding has come from the Queen.

1961

The infants of Queen's Park Primary School in Harlesden, London, concentrate hard on their roles in the school's nativity play.

CHRISTMAS

The Victorians added the Christmas card, the Christmas tree and the idea of giving everyone presents (rather than just the servants on Boxing Day) to the way we celebrate the birth of Christ. All too soon, it was no longer enough for the village choir to rehearse a special Christmas anthem for everyone to listen to in church and then go home to a more special dinner than usual.

While the real meaning of Christmas has become submerged in modern Britain's consumer culture, it is by no means lost. Christmas remains for most people a time for making a special effort to bring families together. Churches are much fuller at Christmas for a range of special services than at any other time of the year except Easter.

For many children, their first introduction to the magic and mystery of the Christmas message comes at school. The infant class's annual performance of the nativity play, in which as many children as possible get a part, remains for many of the children and their parents a lifelong memory.

TODAY

Raymond Briggs's *Snowman* is the theme of this specially decorated shop window, designed to get people into a festive, buying mood.

EISTEDDFODAU IN WALES

The special festivals called eisteddfodau have long held a special place in Welsh cultural life. They celebrate and encourage literature and music, both of which have very long traditions in Wales. Welsh literature, which many believe can be traced back to the Druids, is one of the oldest literatures in Europe.

The first recorded eisteddfod in Wales was in 1176. It was not until the early nineteenth century that the tradition of crowning the best bard of the year began. From this time, too, many rituals purporting to date back to the times of the Druids began to be introduced into the ceremonial of the eisteddfod.

Two particularly important eisteddfodau are held in Wales every year. The Royal National Eisteddfod, held in a different town each year, has competitions in music, singing, prose and poetry in Welsh. The International Music Eisteddfod, held in Llangollen, attracts performers from all over the world.

TODAY

Dr Rowan Williams (right), a fine poet and now Archbishop of Canterbury, was inducted as a Druid at the National Eisteddfod in 2002.

ROYAL DIAMOND JUBILEES

Only two British monarchs have reigned long
enough to celebrate Diamond Jubilees marking
60 years on the throne: Queen Victoria in
1897 and Elizabeth II in 2012. For both, their
Golden Jubilee (50 years) had seen renewed
popularity after periods of questioning and
growth in republican sentiment.

Queen Victoria's Diamond Jubilee was a
time for Imperial pageantry, with leaders of the
countries of the Empire invited to the
celebrations and a splendid six-mile carriage
procession to St Paul's Cathedral. Victoria, by
now quite lame, remained in her carriage for
the brief thanksgiving service, held at the steps
to the cathedral's west door.

A service of thanksgiving, inside St Paul's, was
also the climax of Elizabeth II's Diamond Jubilee
celebrations in June 2012. It came at the end of
four days of celebrations, including a pageant on
the Thames, a public concert in the gardens of
Buckingham Palace and the lighting of over 2,000
beacons across the country and Commonwealth.

PICTURE CREDITS

The publishers would like to thank the following sources for their kind permission to reproduce thepictures in this book:

AKG Images: 76, 90.

Alamy Images: /Peter Bowater: 185; /Greg Balfour Evans: 21; /Elvele Images: 83; /Robert Harding Picture Library: 23; /Rob Whitworth Garden Photography: 27

Billie Love Historical Collection: 52, 114, 146, 148.

The Birmingham Alliance: /Bullring Birmingham opens September 2003. Picture courtesy of the developer, The Birmingham Alliance: 139.

Bubbles Photo Library: /Angela Hampton: 23

Collections: /Phil Crean: 97; /Nigel Hawkins: 55; /Liz Stares: 165

Corbis: /Richard Cummins: 123; /E. O. Hoppé: 182; /Hulton-Deutsch Collection: 168, 230, 182, 184; / Richard Klune: 25; /Chris North/Cordaiy Photo Library: 127; /Michael St. Maur Sheil: 47; /Rudy Sulgan: 135; /Alan Towse/Ecoscene: 104; /Visionhaus: 73; /Patrick Ward: 29.

Ffotograff: /Charles Aithie: 131.

The Francis Frith Collection: 124.

© **FreeFoto.com**: /Ian Britton: 133.

Getty Images: 45, 51, 53, 61, 64, 67, 75, 87, 89, 91, 94, 111, 120, 121, 179, 191; /Bay Hippisley: 167; /Hulton Archive: 12, 18, 20, 24, 30, 42, 79; /, 86, 92, 106, 116, 122, 128, 130, 132, 136, 138, 140, 142, 150; /Clive Mason: 81, 83; /Mark Thompson: 89; /Sion Touhig: 101.

Glasgow City Council: /DRS Graphics/Stephen Hosey: 143.

Lancashire Evening Post: /Iain Lynn: 125.

Mary Evans Picture Library: 190; /Barry Norman: 96.

Ocado: /Ocado in partnership with Waitrose. Photographer: Mike O'Dwyer: 171.

Pictures of Britain: /Deryck L. Hallam: 137; / Bernard Humphries: 117; /Julian Worker: 43

Press Association Images: /Mike Egerton: 97; / Stefan Rousseau: 181

Rex Features: /Nigel R. Barklie: 157 /David Bebber: 19; /Adrian Brooks: 151; /Denis Cameron: 187; /Mark Campbell: 13; /Clive Dixon: 15, 33; /David Fisher: 31; / Richard Gardner: 107; /Nils Jorgensen: 29; /Robert Judges: 153; /Tom Kidd: 101; /Herbie Knott: 93; /Tony Kyriacou: 183; /Jeroen Oerlemans: 177; /Peter Price: 147; /Brian Rasic: 85; /Tim Rooke: 71; /SIPA Press: 169; /South West News: 109; /Jeremy Sutton Hibbert: 161; /Ray Tang: 41, 49; /Andrew Terrill: 105; /TimePix/Margaret Bourke-White: 48; /Times Newspapers Ltd: 149

Royal Botanic Gardens, Kew: 32

Scottish Viewpoint: /Wattie Cheung: 163; /Drew Farrell: 69; /Colin McPherson: 57; /Paul Tomkins/ VisitScotland: 35, 77.

Nigel Sutton: 155

Topfoto.co.uk: 1, 2, 6tl, 6tr, 6bl, 6br, 8, 14, 16, 22, 26, 28, 34, 38, 39, 40, 44, 50, 58, 66, 68, 74, 78, 82, 88, 97, 100, 110, 112, 113,126, 134, 152, 154, 156, 158, 159, 160, 162, 164, 166, 170, 174, 178, 180, 186, 188, 189; /Stewart Galloway: 10-11, 36-37, 62-63, 98-99, 118-119, 144-145, 172-173; /HIP: 60, 72, 102; /HIP/Museum of London: 56; / HIP/National Motor Museum: 8tl, 54, 80; /PA Photos: 46, 59, 95, 115,141, 175; /Ponopresse: 108; /PressNet: 17, 84; /Ray Roberts: 103; /UPPA: 61, 71, 129

Every effort has been made to acknowledge correctly and contact the source and/or copyright holder of each picture and Carlton Books Limited apologises for any unintentional errors or omissions which will be corrected in future editions of this book.

PUBLISHING CREDITS

Art Director: Lucy Coley
Art Editor: Vicky Holmes
Project Editor: Amie McKee
Design: Brian Flynn
Editorial: Rob Dimery
Picture research: Adrian Bentley and Steve Behan
Production: Lucy Woodhead and Janette Burgin